100 Any-Size Christmas Quilt Blocks

by Rita Weiss & Linda Causee

Before You Start

Choose the block you want to make. Inside this book, you will find a self-loading CD that contains 100 Christmas quilt block patterns in several sizes. There are blocks that use foundation piecing, appliqué or patchwork templates. The files on the CD are easily opened using Adobe® Reader®. If you don't have Adobe® Reader® on your computer you can get a free download at http://www.adobe.com/. The site provides easy, step-by-step instructions for the download.

When you are ready to make your quilt, simply print out the required pattern(s) for your block(s). If you choose a foundation-pieced or appliqué block, print out the pattern in the size you desire: 4", 5", 6", 7" or 8". If you would like to make a 10" block, you will need to visit your local copy store and enlarge a 5" block by 200% then print it out on 11" x 17" paper. If you choose a patchwork block (4", 6", 8", 10", 12" or 16"), print out the templates needed for your block, then glue the templates on to plastic or heavy cardboard. When you are certain that your glue has dried, cut out your templates. If your templates become worn, simply repeat the process.

LEISURE ARTS, INC.
Maumelle, Arkansas

Produced by

Production Team

Creative Directors:	Jean Leinhauser and Rita Weiss
Book Design:	Linda Causee
Technical Editor:	Ann Harnden
Block Diagrams:	April McArthur

We have made every effort to ensure that these instructions are accurate and complete. We cannot, however, be responsible for human error, typographical mistakes or variations in individual work.

Published by Leisure Arts, Inc.

© 2014 by Leisure Arts, Inc.

104 Champs Boulevard, STE. 100

Maumelle, AR 72113

www. leisurearts.com

ISBN: 978-1-4647-1592-1

Library of Congress Control Number: 2014940372

Contents

Introduction

If you enjoy decorating your house at the Christmas holiday season, then we can't imagine not using quilts or quilt designs to add something special to your home.

In this book we've given you a collection of holiday designs made with quilt blocks. Use them to make quilts to cover all the beds in your house on Christmas morning. Santa, himself, will be amazed!

Look through the pages of blocks and choose your favorites. You can create an entire quilt by repeating one block, or elect to make a sampler quilt or wall hanging with many different blocks. Either way you'll create a wonderful warm holiday tradition to hand down to your children or grandchildren: a quilt that's used only for Christmas.

If, however, making full-size bed quilts is too large a task, why not plan to decorate your house with smaller projects that have a Christmas theme? We've even given you instructions for making some Christmas placemats as well as several small wall hangings to decorate your house at the holiday season.

In this book, you'll find that there are three different kinds of blocks: blocks that use templates, blocks that use foundation piecing and blocks that use applique. If you are an experienced quilter, or just a beginner, you may agree that one of the most difficult parts of a project is finding the necessary patterns or templates, no matter which technique you choose.

Find the answer to that problem in this book and its enclosed CD! For applique and foundation piecing designs, just place the CD into your computer, click on the block of your choice in the size that you want and print out the patterns you'll need. For traditional patchwork designs, print out the templates you need for one of the available block sizes and glue them onto plastic or heavy cardboard. If your original templates become worn, or if you need additional pieces, just repeat the process.

If you've forgotten—or if you've never learned how to make a quilt, we've included some basic instructions on the CD.

So get ready to add a colorful addition to your holiday decorations. Make a miniature quilt, a wall hanging, or even a full-size bed quilt, and then be prepared to receive applause from all who visit your home over the holidays.

Trumpeting Angel

Foundation Piecing

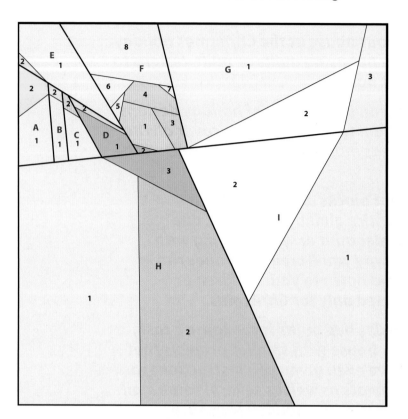

Christmas Flower

Foundation Piecing

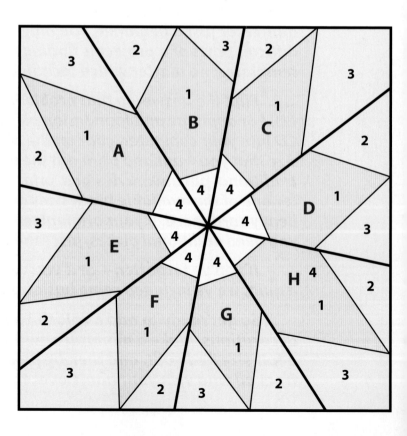

Christmas Tree
Foundation Piecing

2	E 1	3
2	D 1	3
2	C 1	3
2	B 1	3
5	A 4	6
2	1	3

Noel
Foundation Piecing

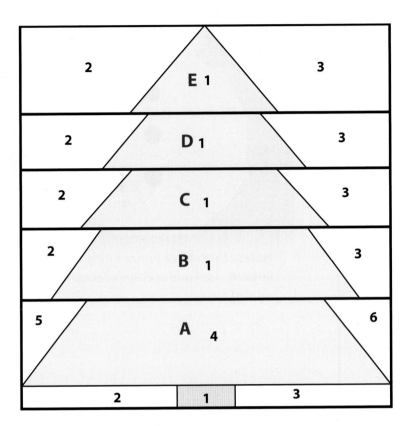

Snowman
Foundation Piecing

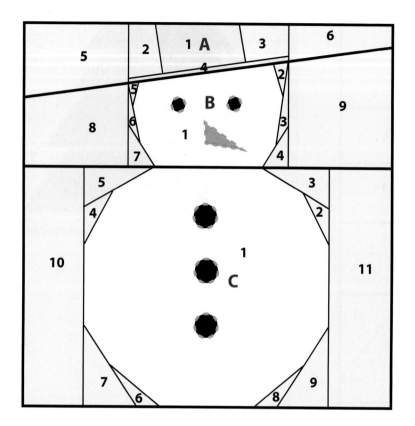

Note: *Attach black buttons for eyes and buttons. Appliqué or embroider carrot-shaped nose.*

Star of Bethlehem
Foundation Piecing

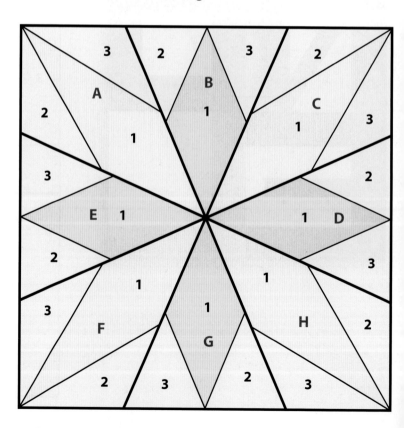

Snow-tipped Pine

Foundation Piecing

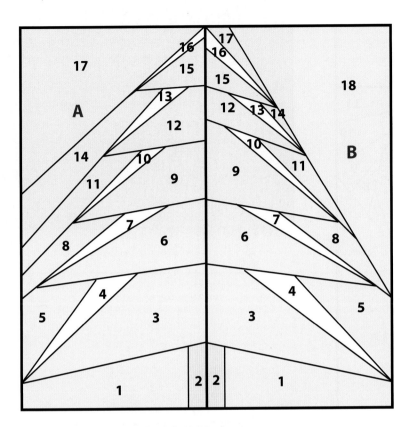

Santa Claus

Foundation Piecing

Note: *Use buttons, embroidery or applique for facial features. Use a pompon or appliqué for tip of Santa's hat.*

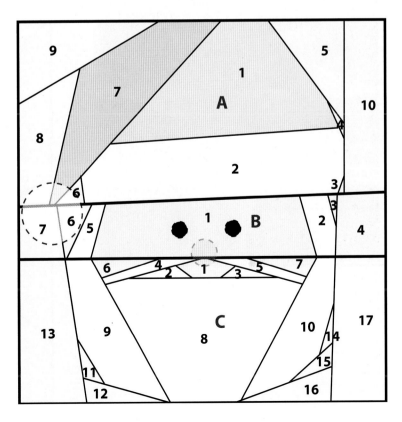

Teardrop Ornament

Foundation Piecing

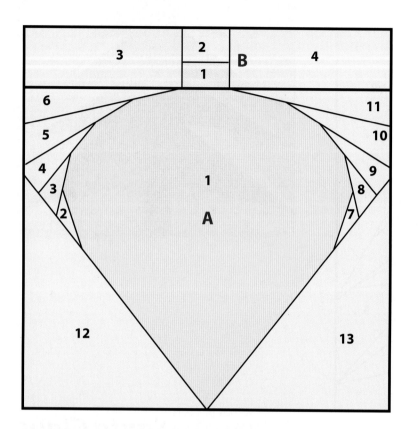

Dimensional Star

Foundation Piecing

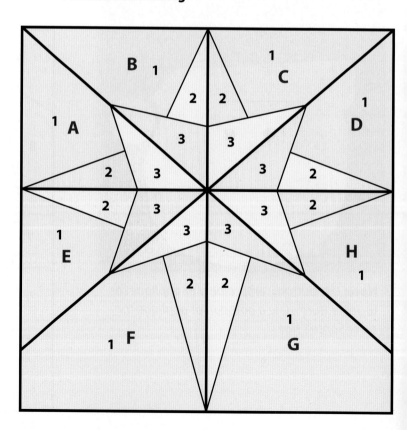

Christmas Present
Foundation Piecing

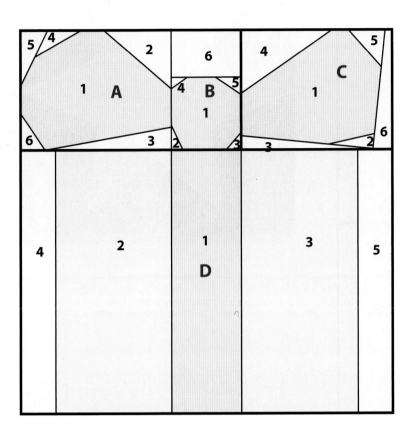

A
5 4
2
1
6
3

B
6
4 1 5
2 3

C
4 5
1
6
2 3
3

D
4 2 1 3 5

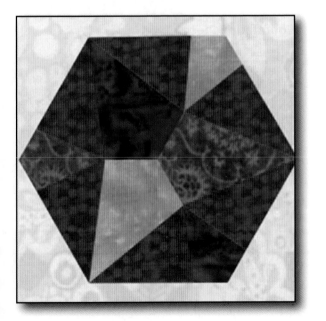

Tumbling Christmas Trees
Foundation Piecing

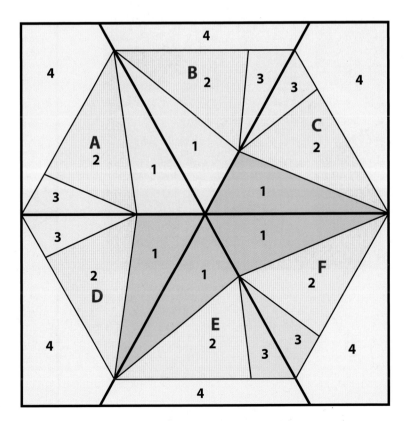

A 2
B 2
C 2
D 2
E 2
F 2

4

9

Six-point Star

Foundation Piecing

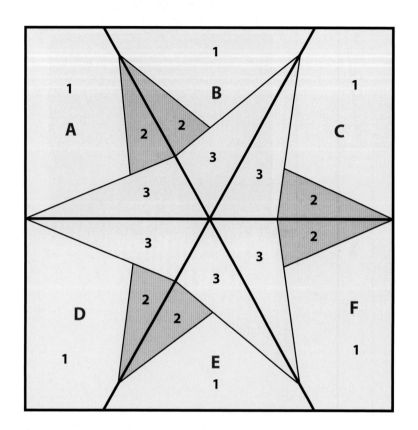

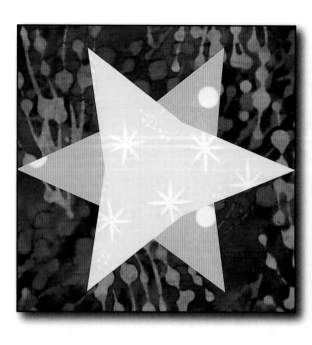

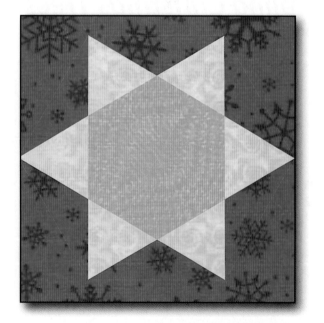

Star of David

Foundation Piecing

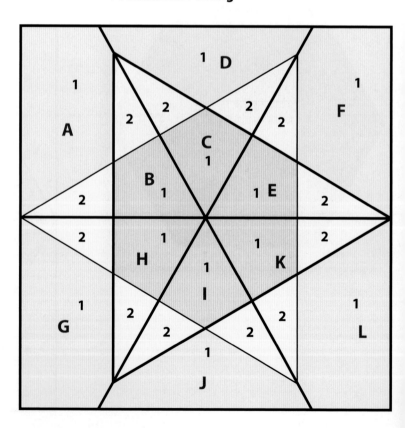

Christmas Candle
Foundation Piecing

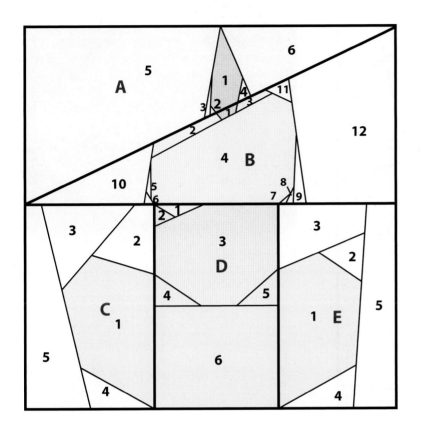

Christmas Candle foundation piecing pattern with sections A, B, C, D, E and numbered pieces 1–12.

Christmas Stocking
Foundation Piecing

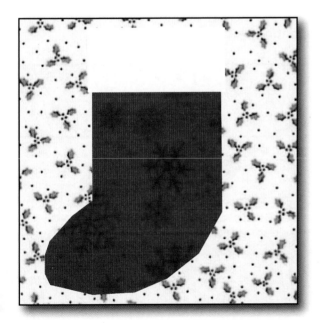

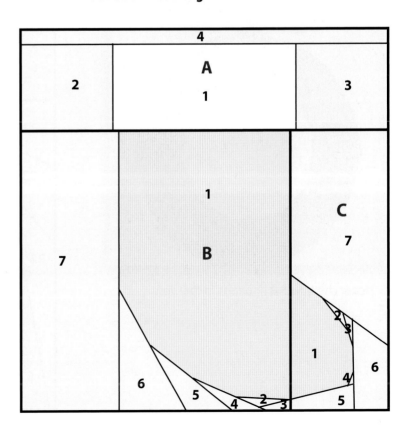

Christmas Stocking foundation piecing pattern with sections A, B, C and numbered pieces.

Golden Bell

Foundation Piecing

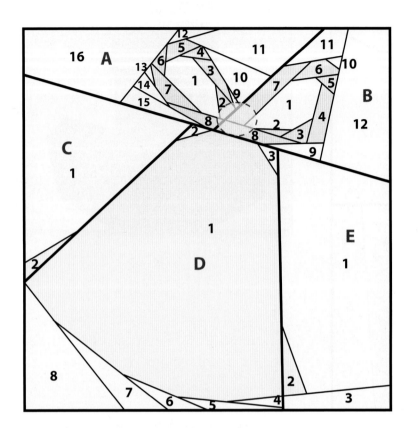

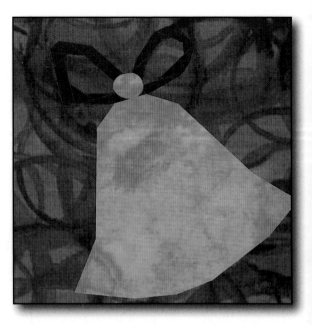

Christmas Wreath

Foundation Piecing

Note: *Use buttons or beads for berries.*

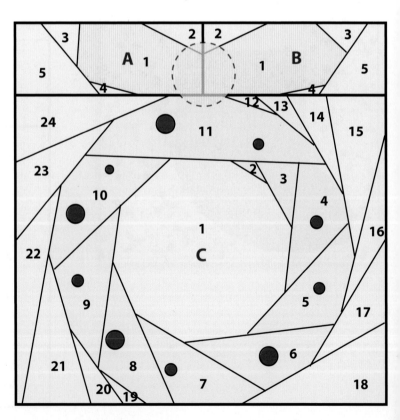

Happy Reindeer
Foundation Piecing

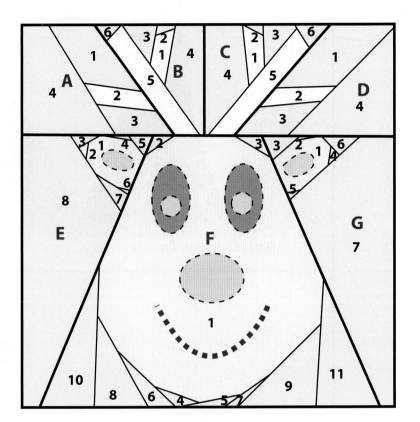

Note: *Appliqué inner ears, eyes and nose; embroider smile.*

Flying Angel
Foundation Piecing

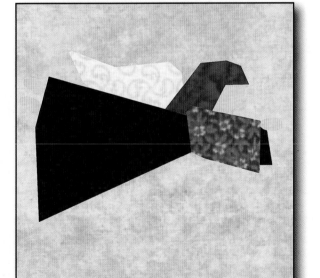

Praying Angel
Foundation Piecing

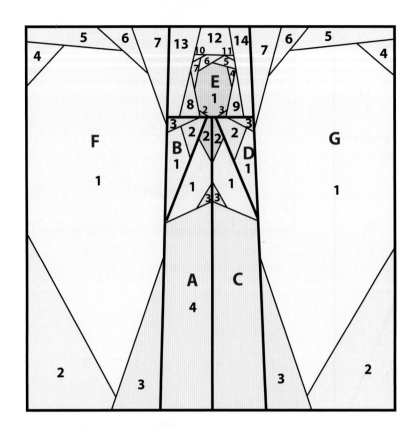

Note: *Embroider facial features*

Shiny Ornament
Foundation Piecing

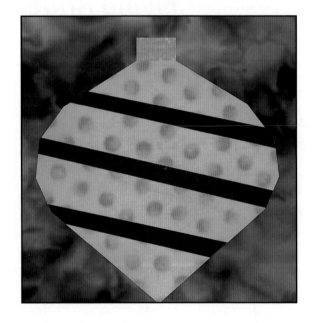

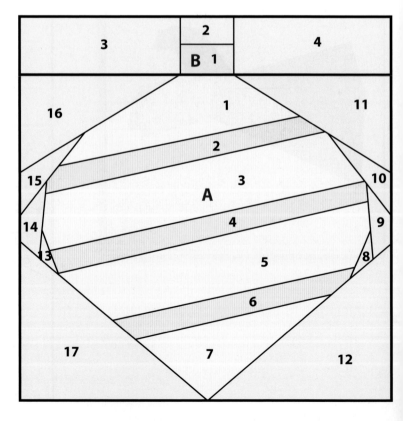

Santa's Sleigh
Foundation Piecing

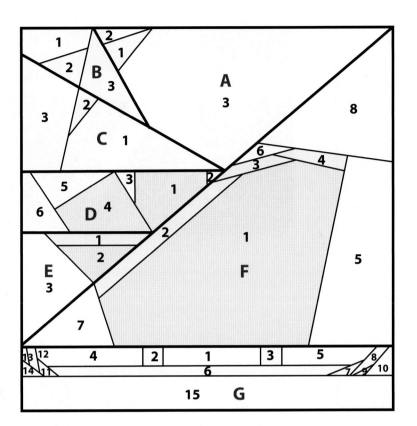

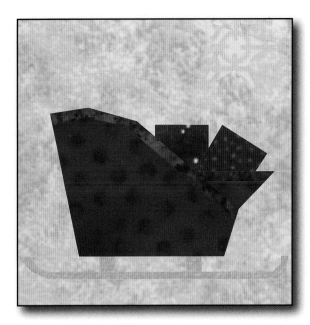

Tumbling Snowflake
Foundation Piecing

Snowflake

Foundation Piecing

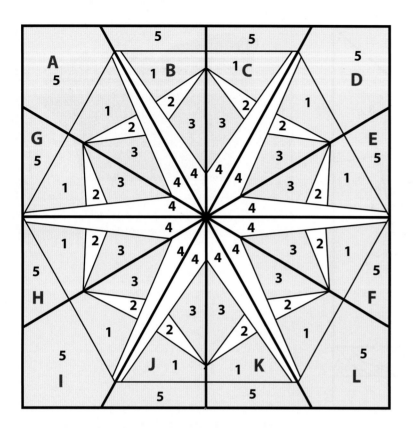

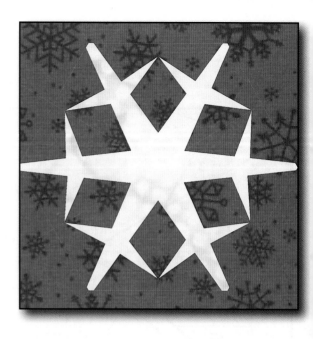

Log Cabin Tree

Foundation Piecing

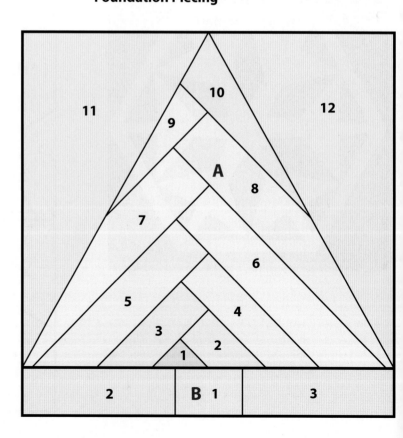

Log Cabin Ornament

Foundation Piecing

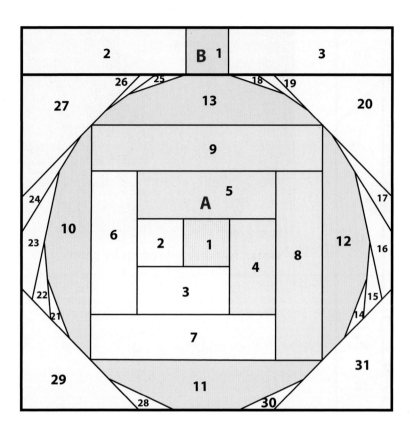

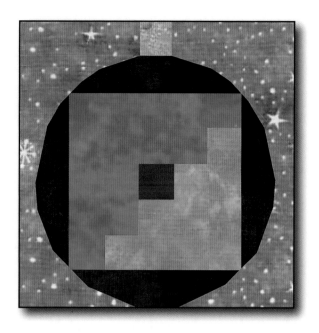

		B 1		
2			3	

26 25   18 19

27   13   20

9

24

A   5

10   6   2   1   17

23

8   12   16

22   3   4

21   15

7   14

29   31

11

28   30

Log Cabin Stocking

Foundation Piecing

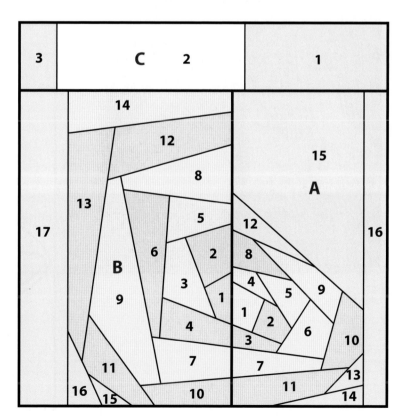

3	C	2	1

14

12

8

13   15

17   5   A

6   2   12

B   3   1   8

9   4   9

4   1   5

4   2   6   10

3

7   3

7

11   13

16   11   14

15   10

Log Cabin Wreath

Foundation Piecing

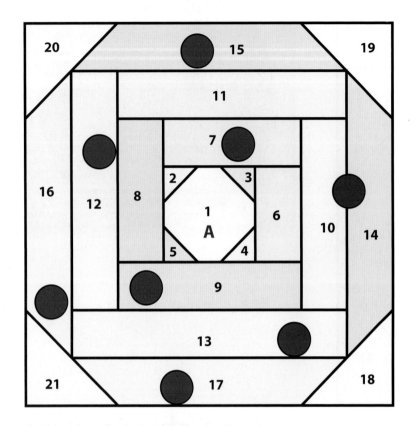

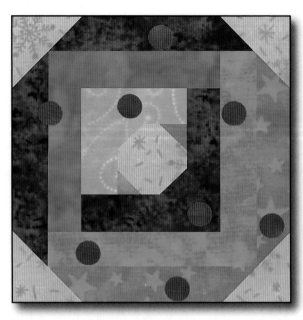

Note: *Use buttons or beads for berries.*

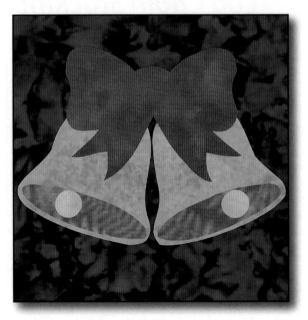

Christmas Bells

Appliqué

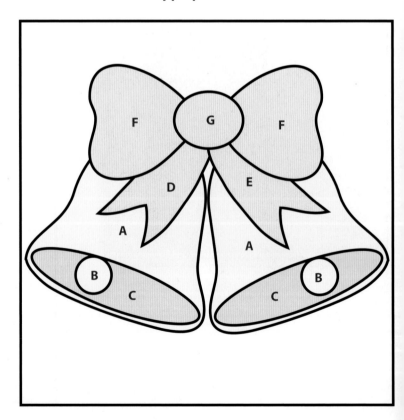

Holly Wreath
Appliqué

Note: *Use buttons or beads for berries.*

Christmas Lights
Appliqué

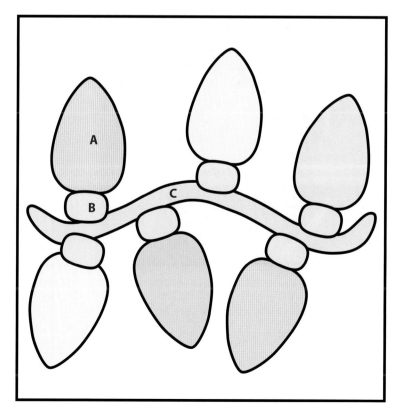

Glowing Angel

Appliqué

Gingerbread Man

Appliqué

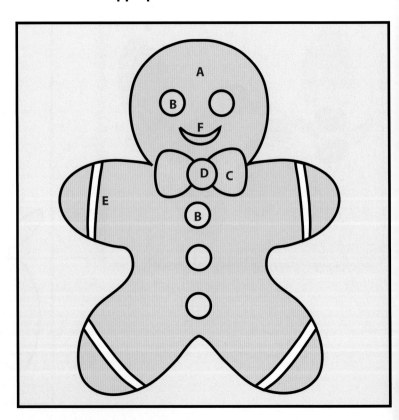

Ho Ho Ho Santa

Appliqué

Bubble Ornament

Appliqué

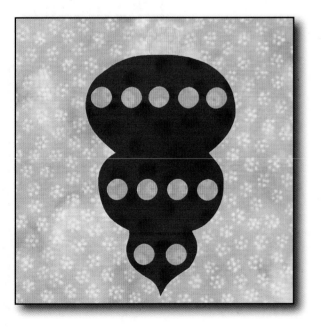

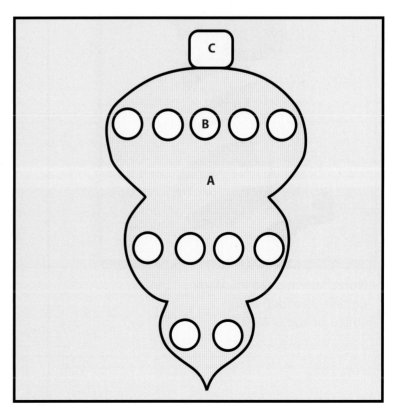

Starburst
Appliqué

Elf Stocking
Appliqué

Note: Pattern is the stocking pattern. Appliqué white stripes on top of A.

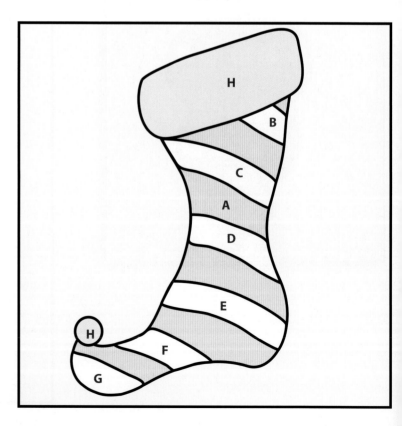

Topsy Turvy Snowman

Appliqué

Note: *Appliqué or embroider face and buttons. Buttons can also be used if desired.*

Jesus is Born

Appliqué

Christmas Candy

Appliqué

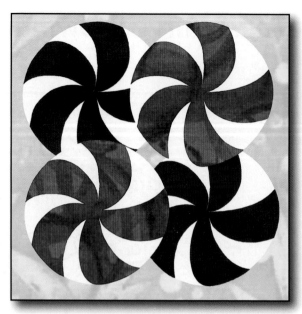

Note: *Pattern A is a full circle. Appliqué red or green sections to A.*

Beaded Tree

Appliqué

Note: *Use buttons or beads for ornaments if desired.*

Diamond Ornament

Appliqué

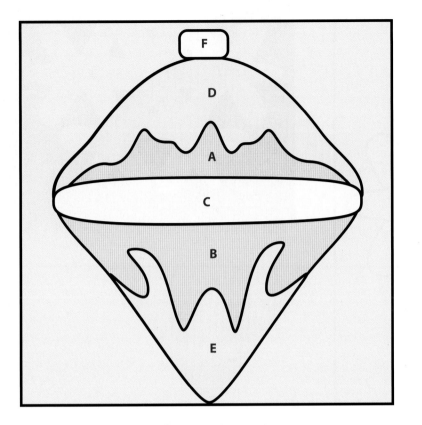

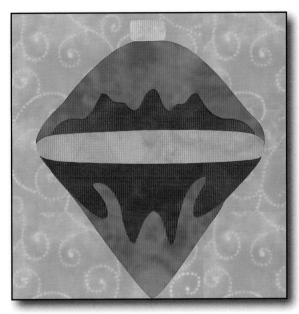

Note: *Use red beads for the berries on the holly leaves.*

Waiting for Santa

Appliqué

Pretty Snowflake

Appliqué

Note: *Use beads or buttons for pattern D if desired.*

Poinsettia Appliqué

Appliqué

26

Candy Cane

Appliqué

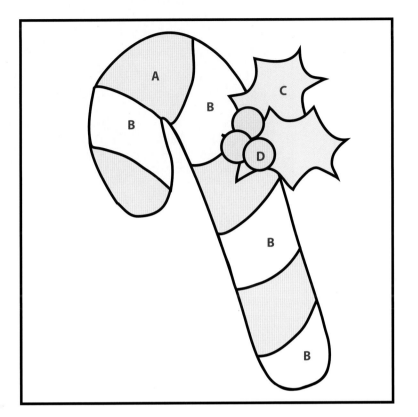

Notes: *Pattern A is the candy cane shape. Appliqué the white stripes on top of A. Use beads or buttons in place of D circles if desired.*

Holly Trim

Appliqué

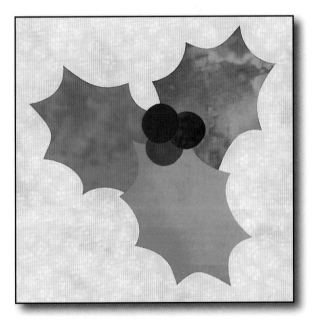

Simple Poinsettia

Appliqué

Note: *Use beads or buttons for C circles.*

Note: *Use buttons or beads for D ornaments if desired.*

Star-topped Tree

Appliqué

Bethlehem Star 2

Patchwork

Bow Knot

Patchwork

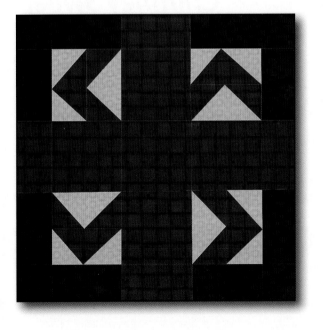

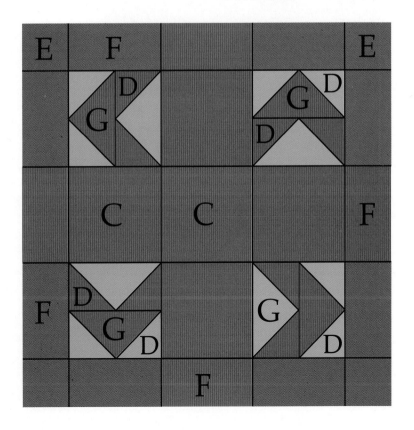

King's Camel

Patchwork

Chimney Sweep

Patchwork

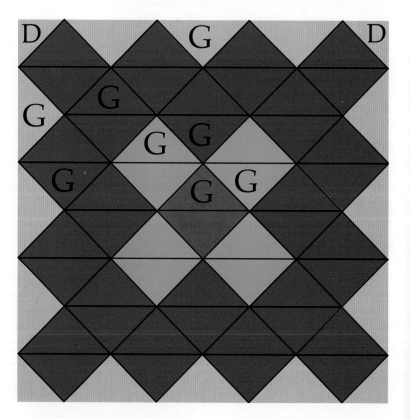

Christmas Bouquet

Patchwork

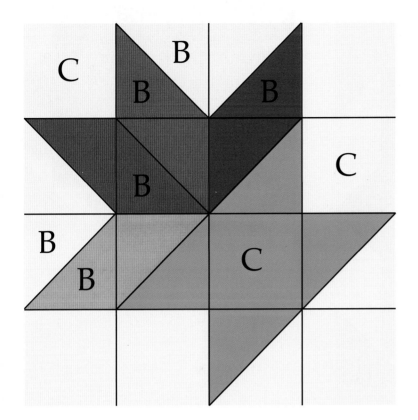

Christmas Cactus

Patchwork

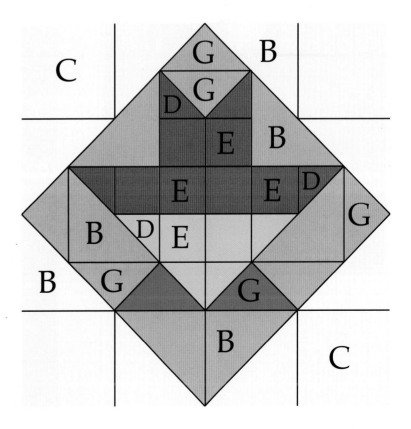

Christmas Cards
Patchwork

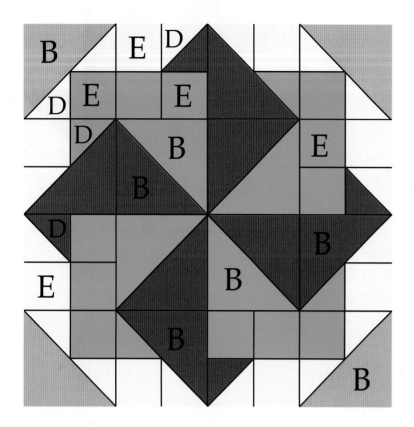

Christmas Church
Patchwork

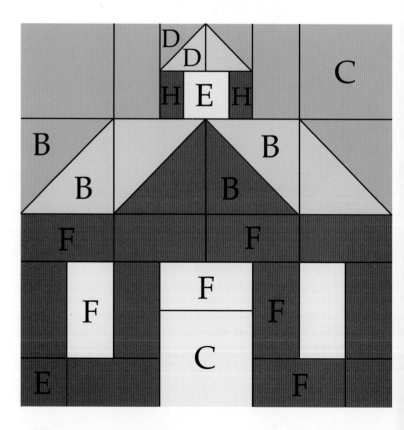

Christmas Goose

Patchwork

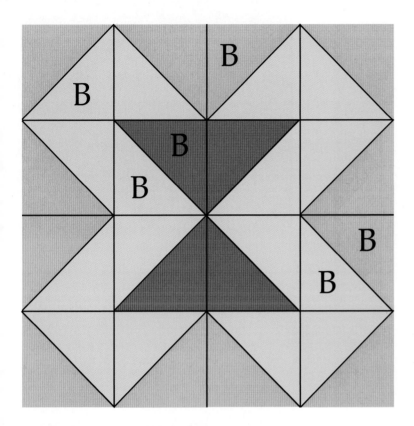

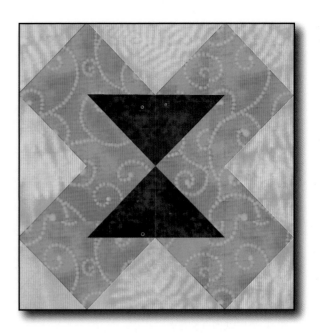

Christmas Ivy

Patchwork

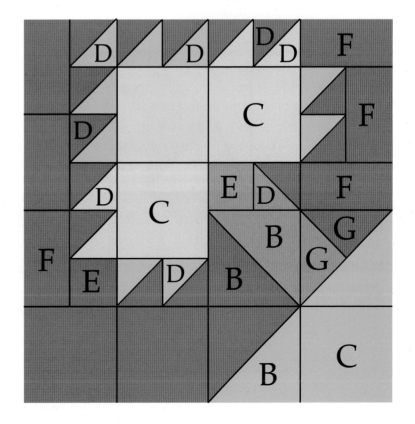

Christmas Laurel Wreath
Patchwork

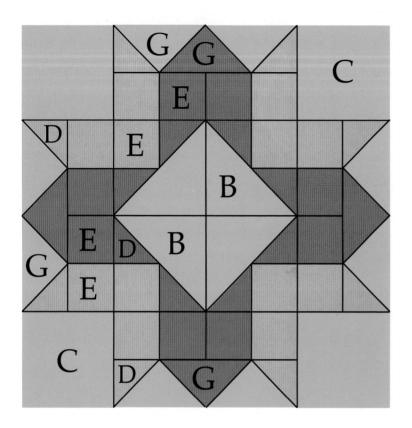

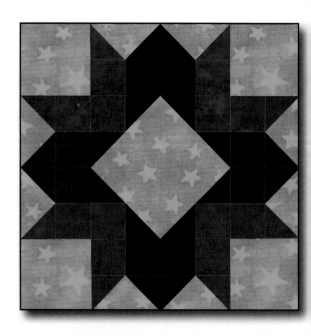

Christmas Lilies
Patchwork

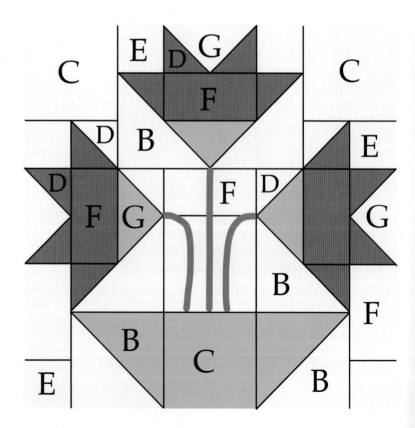

Note: *Appliqué stems at base of flowers.*

Christmas Patch Blossom Tree

Patchwork

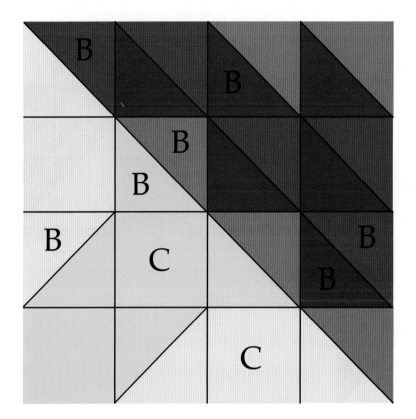

Christmas Pine Tree

Patchwork

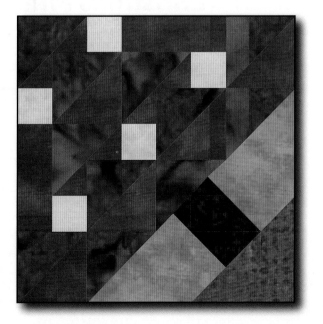

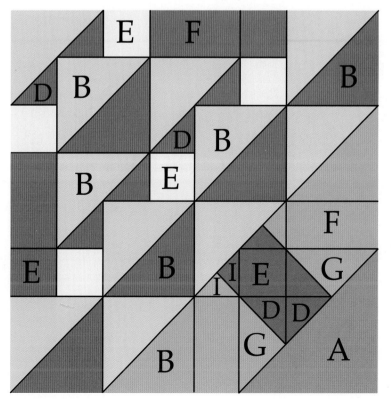

Christmas Evergreen Tree
Patchwork

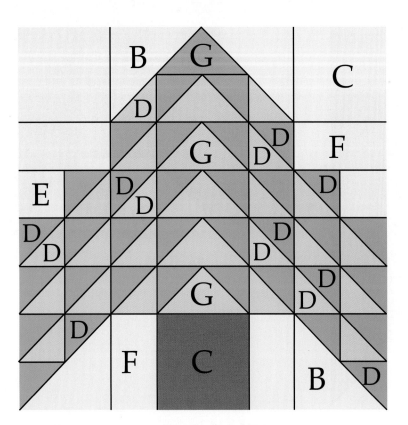

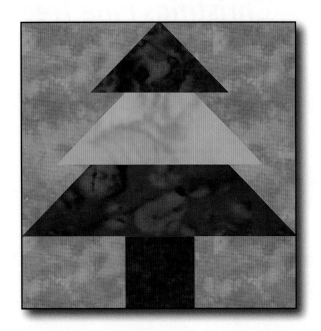

Christmas Pine
Patchwork

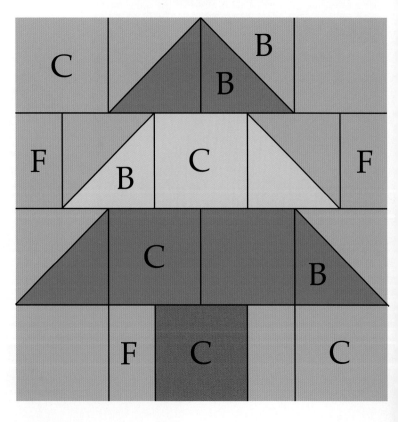

Christmas Snow Crystals
Patchwork

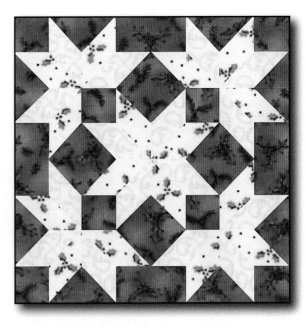

Christmas Star
Patchwork

Fan Tree
Patchwork

Squatty Tree
Patchwork

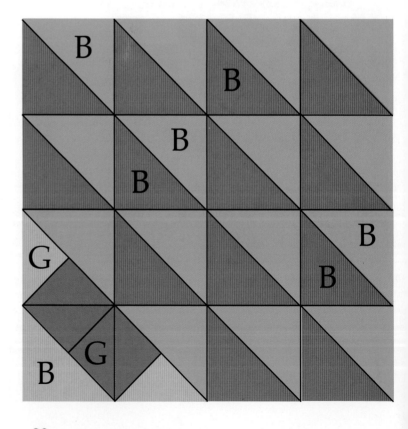

Polka Dot Tree
Patchwork

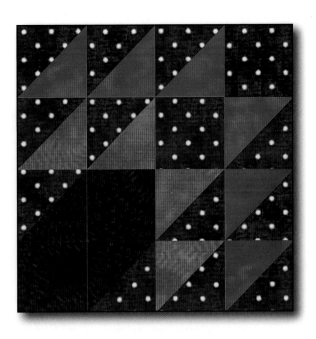

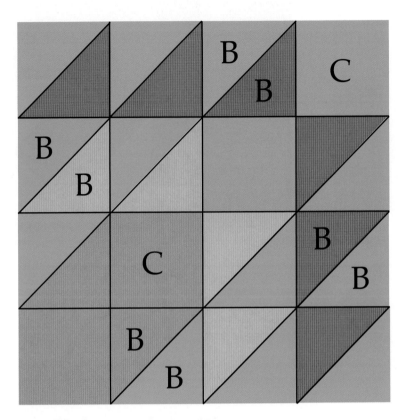

Four-Patch Tree
Patchwork

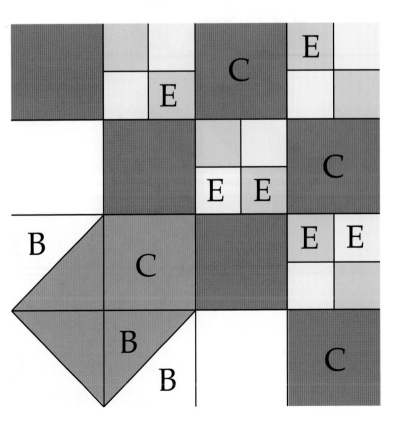

Flame Tree
Patchwork

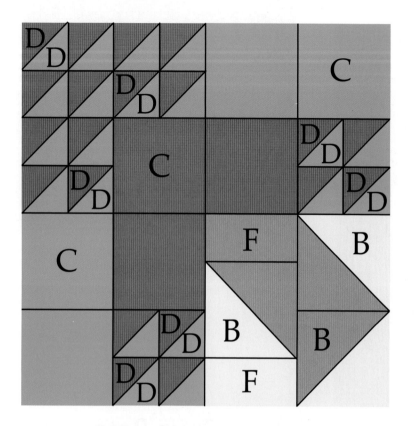

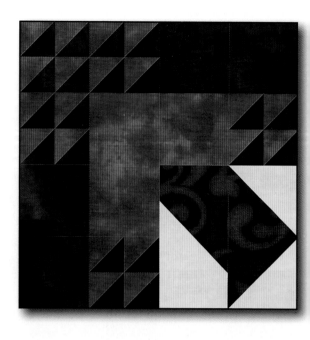

Patchwork Tree
Patchwork

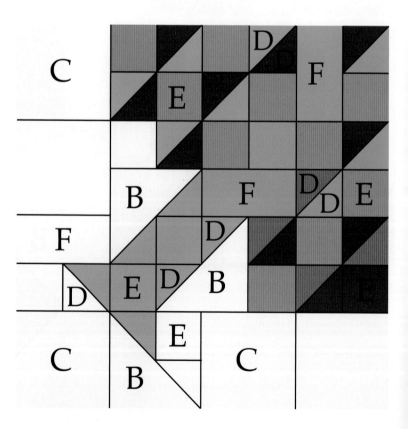

Tall Tree

Patchwork

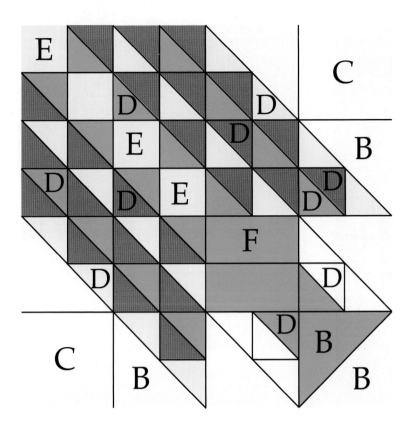

Cottage Tree

Patchwork

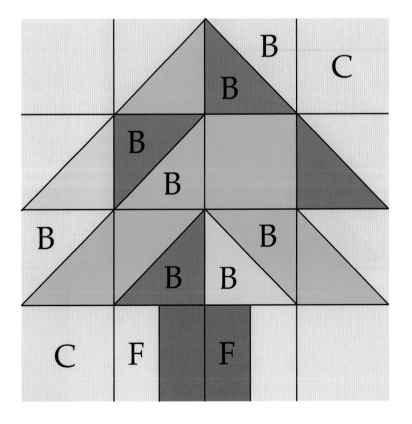

Topiary Tree

Patchwork

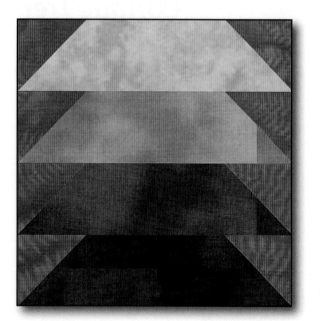

Christmas Tree Everlasting

Patchwork

Elegant Tree

Patchwork

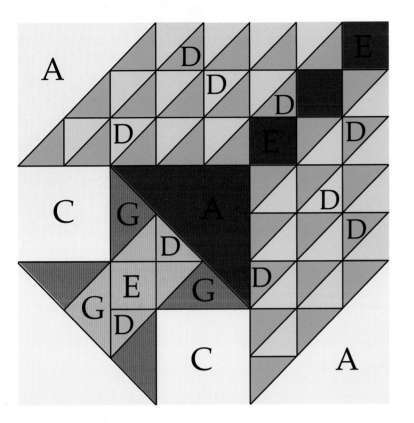

Diamond Wreath

Patchwork

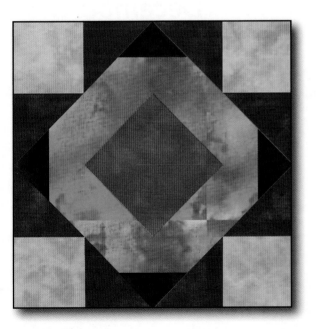

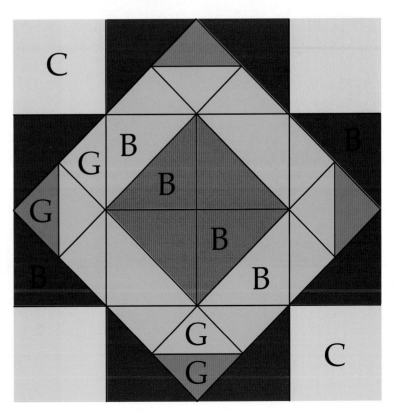

Star Wreath
Patchwork

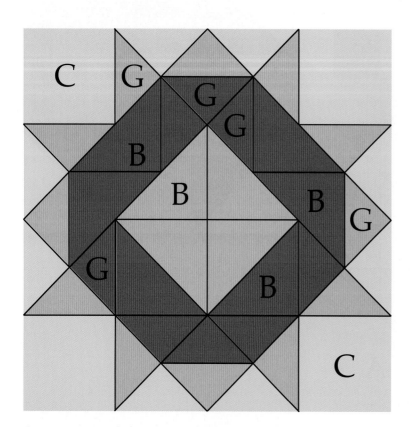

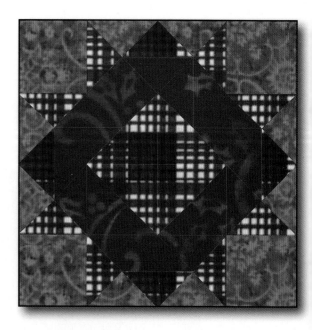

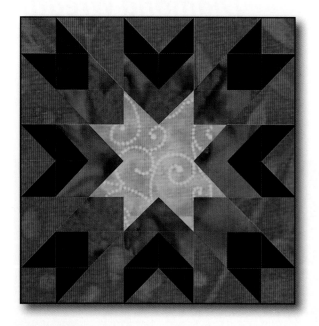

December Star
Patchwork

Georgetown Christmas Wreath

Patchwork

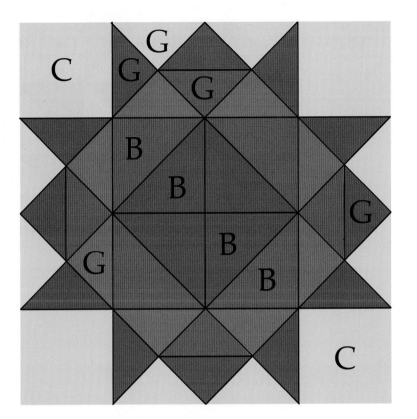

Home for Christmas

Patchwork

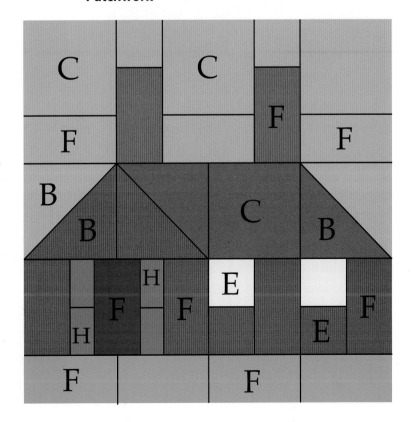

Ladies Christmas Wreath

Patchwork

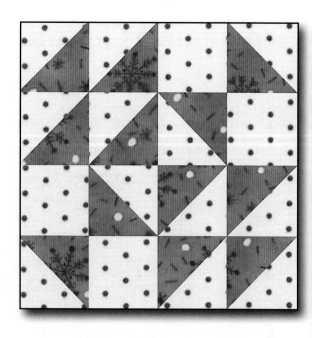

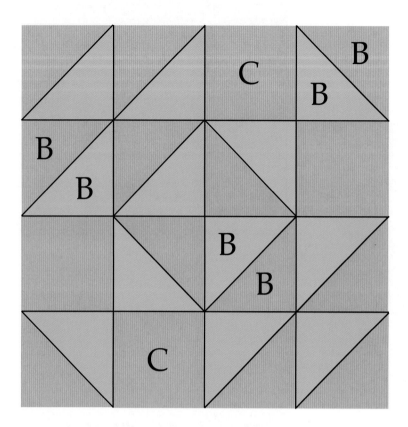

Old Snowflake

Patchwork

Open Gift Box

Patchwork

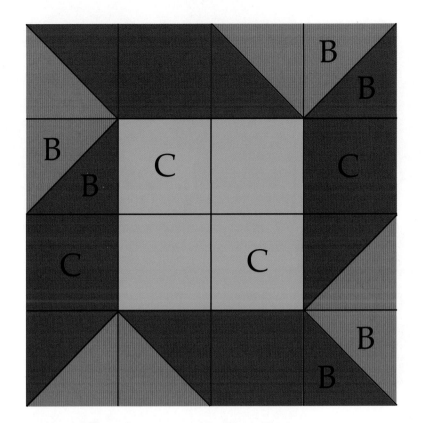

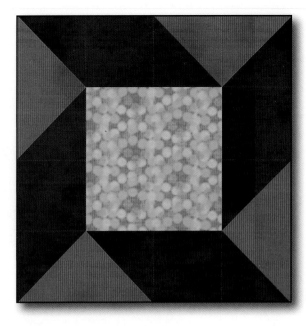

Package Bows

Patchwork

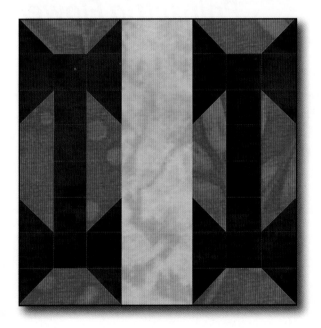

Poinsettia Cross
Patchwork

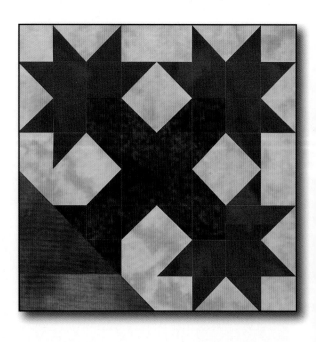

Poinsettia Flower
Patchwork

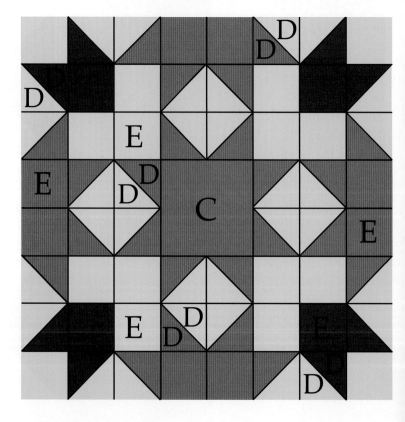

Double Poinsettia

Patchwork

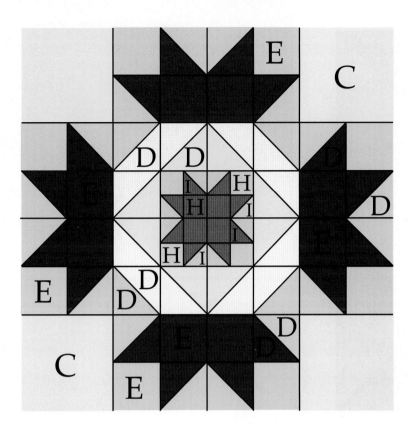

Poinsettia Cluster

Patchwork

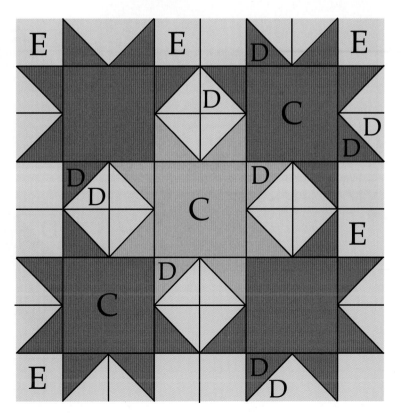

Ribbon Border

Patchwork

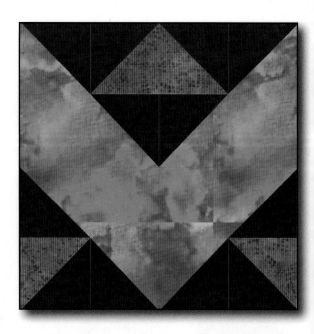

Ribbon Bow

Patchwork

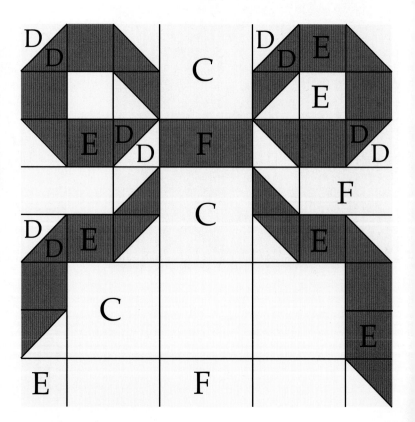

Ribbons

Patchwork

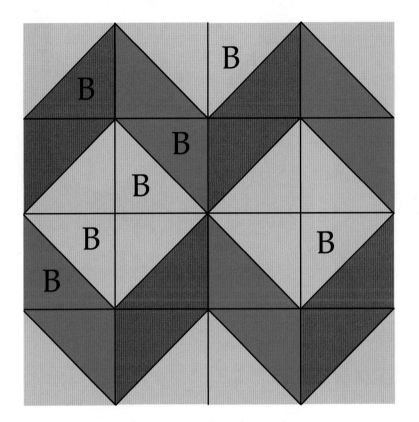

Santa's Starry Path

Patchwork

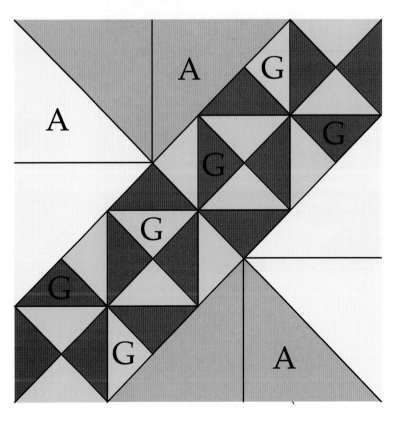

Snowballs

Patchwork

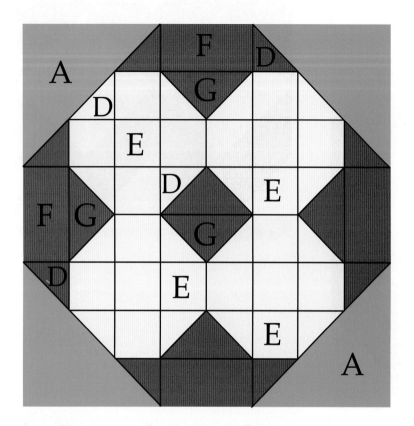

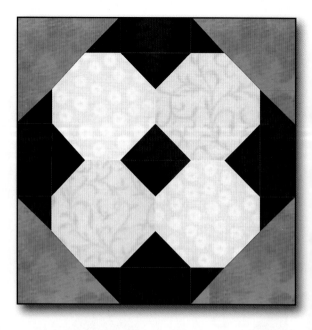

Star of the Magi

Patchwork

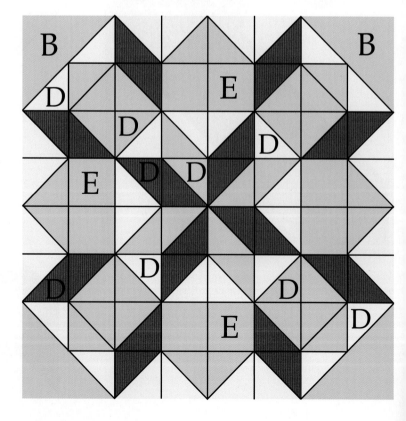

Zigzag Tree

Patchwork

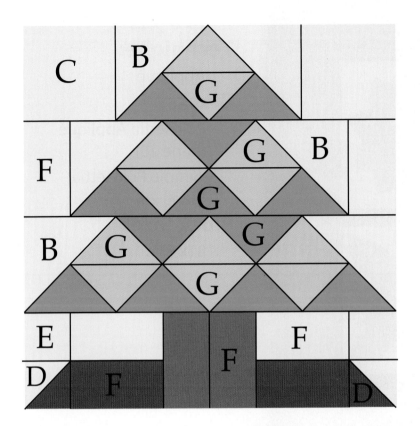

Buckeye Bow

Patchwork

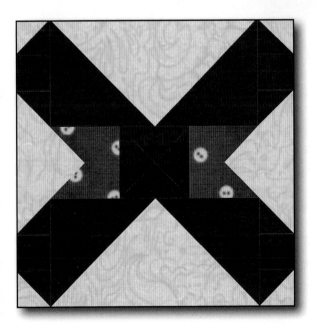

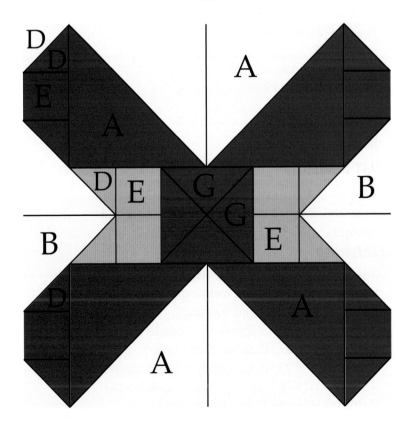

Poinsettia Path

Appliqué

Approximate Size:
25 ½" x 25 ½"

Technique:
Appliqué

Blocks:
Poinsettia Appliqué (page 26)
Simple Poinsettia (page 28)

Block Size:
8" x 8"

MATERIALS:
½ yard light yellow
¼ yard red
¼ yard burgundy
fat quarter dark yellow
¼ yard green
¾ yard backing
Batting

CUTTING:
Blocks
4 squares, 8 ½" x 8 ½", light yellow (background square)

Finishing
2 strips, 1 ½" x 8 ½", red (sashing)
3 strips, 1 ½" x 17 ½", red (sashing)
2 strips, 1 ½" x 19 ½", red (sashing)
2 strips, 2 ½" x 19 ½", green (first border)
2 strips, 2 ½" x 23 ½", green (first border)
2 strips, 1 ½" x 23 ½", burgundy (second border)
2 strips, 1 ½" x 25 ½", burgundy (second border)
3 strips, 2 ½"-wide, burgundy (binding)

INSTRUCTIONS:
1. Prepare poinsettia petals, leaves and centers according to your favorite Appliqué method on the enclosed CD. Make two of each block.

2. Referring to photo, sew two blocks together with a 1 ½" x 8" red sashing strip in between. Repeat.

3. Sew the rows of blocks together with a 1 ½" x 17 ½" red sashing strip in between. Sew the remaining 1 ½" x 17 ½" red sashing strips to the sides of the quilt top.

4. Sew the 1 ½" x 19 ½" red sashing strips to the top and bottom of the quilt.

5. Sew first and second borders to quilt top sides first, then top and bottom.

6. Finish quilt referring to Finishing your Quilt on the CD.

Christmas Treats
Appliqué

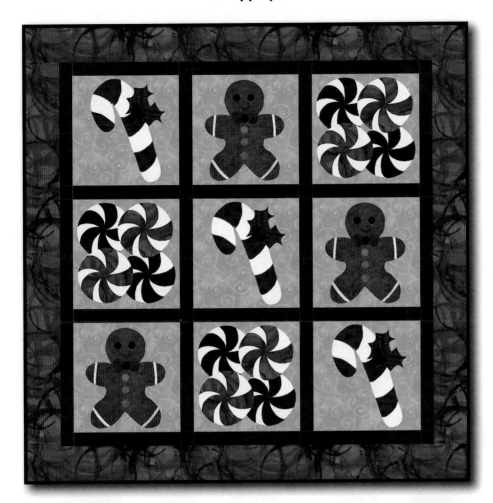

Approximate Size:
34 ½" x 34 ½"
Technique:
Appliqué
Blocks:
Candy Cane
(page 27)
Gingerbread Man
(page 20)
Christmas Candy
(page 24)
Block Size:
8" x 8"

MATERIALS
1 yard light green
¼ yard red
½ yard burgundy
½ yard med green
1 yard dark green
¼ yard brown
½ yard white
1 yard backing
Batting

CUTTING:
Blocks
9 squares, 8 ½" x 8 ½", light green (background square)
Finishing
6 strips, 1 ½" x 8 ½", burgundy (sashing)
4 strips, 1 ½" x 26 ½", burgundy (sashing)
2 strips, 1 ½" x 28 ½", burgundy (sashing)
2 strips, 2 ½" x 19 ½", dk green (border)
2 strips, 2 ½" x 23 ½", dk green (border)
4 strips, 2 ½"-wide, burgundy (binding)

INSTRUCTIONS:
1. Prepare appliqué pieces for the Gingerbread Man, Candy Cane and Christmas Candy blocks according to your favorite Appliqué method on the enclosed CD. Make three of each block.

2. Referring to photo, sew three blocks together with 1 ½" x 8 ½" burgundy sashing strips in between blocks. Repeat for two more rows.

3. Sew the rows of blocks together with 1 ½" x 26 ½" burgundy sashing strips in between rows. Sew the remaining 1 ½" x 26 ½" burgundy sashing strips to the sides of the quilt top.

4. Sew the 1 ½" x 28 ½" burgundy sashing strips to the top and bottom of the quilt.

5. Sew border to quilt top sides first, then top and bottom.

6. Finish quilt referring to Finishing your Quilt on the CD.

Santa's Starry Path Twin Size Quilt

Patchwork

Approximate Size:

86 ½" x 110 ½"

Technique:

Patchwork

Block:

Santa's Starry Path
(page 51)

Block Size:

12" x 12"

MATERIALS

3 yards green
3 yards red
2 yards beige
2 yards beige holly print
9 yards backing
Batting

CUTTING:

Blocks

192 A Triangles, beige
192 A Triangles, beige holly print
672 G Triangles, red
672 G Triangles, green

Finishing

10 strips, 2 ½"-wide, red (first border)
12 strips, 5 ½"-wide, green (second border)
12 strips, 2 ½"-wide, red (binding)

INSTRUCTIONS:

Santa's Starry Path Block

1. Sew a beige A triangle to a beige holly print triangle A. Sew a beige A triangle and a beige holly print triangle A to square just made. Repeat for another triangle.

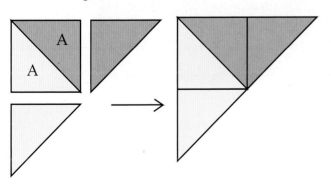

2. Sew a red G triangle to a green G triangle. Repeat for 14 pairs of triangles.

3. Sew two pairs of G triangles together to complete a pieced square. Repeat for four pieced squares.

4. Sew pieced squares and triangles together from steps 2 and 3 to form a diagonal band.

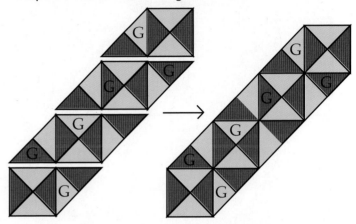

5. Sew pieced triangles from step 1 to opposite sides of diagonal band to complete block.

make 48 Blocks

6. Make a total of 48 blocks.

Finishing

1. Referring to photo, sew blocks together in eight rows of six blocks each. Note position of blocks.

2. Sew rows together.

3. Attach first and second borders sides first, then to the top and bottom of quilt top.

4. Finish quilt referring to Finishing your Quilt on the CD.

Star of the Magi Lap Quilt

Patchwork

Approximate Size:
52 ½" x 64 ½"
Technique:
Patchwork
Block:
Star of the Magi
(page 52)
Block Size:
12" x 12"

MATERIALS
2 yards dark green
4 yards medium green
2 yards red
4 yards backing
Batting

CUTTING:
Blocks
48 B triangles, dark green
288 D triangles, red
432 D triangles, dark green
432 D triangles, medium green
96 E Squares, dark green

Finishing
8 strips, 2 ½"-wide, red (first border)
10 strips, 6 ½"-wide, medium green (second border)
10 strips, 2 ½"-wide, dark green (binding)

INSTRUCTIONS:
Star of the Magi Blocks
1. Sew medium and dark green D triangles to make a pieced triangle; sew to dark green B triangle for Unit 1. Sew red, medium green, and dark green triangles and a dark green E square together for Units 2 and 3. For unit 4, sew red, medium green and dark green D triangles. Make 4 of each unit.

2. Place units together in rows of four blocks.

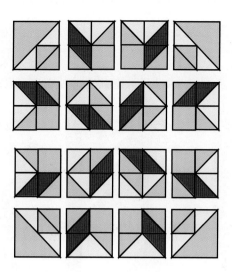

3. Sew units together in rows, then sew rows together.

Make a total of 12 Star of the Magi blocks.

Finishing
1. Referring to photo, sew blocks together in four rows of three blocks each.

2. Sew rows together.

3. Attach first and second borders sides first, then to the top and bottom of quilt top.

4. Finish quilt referring to Finishing your Quilt on the CD.

Christmas Tree Farm

Patchwork, Appliqué, and Foundation Piecing

Approximate Size:

39 ½" x 39 ½"

Techniques:

Foundation Piecing, Patchwork
and Applique

Block Size:

8" x 8"

Blocks:

Snow-tipped Tree (page 7)

Zigzag Tree (page 53)

Beaded Tree (page 24)

Topiary Tree (page 42)

Christmas Tree (page 5)

Cottage Tree (page 41)

Star-topped Tree (page 28)

Christmas Pine Tree (page 36)

Log Cabin Tree (page 16)

MATERIALS

¾ yard light blue

½ yard each of assorted light, medium and dark greens

fat quarter each yellow, red, brown

1 yard dark green (sashing, border and binding)

½ yard medium green (border)

1 ¼ yards backing

Batting

foundation paper

CUTTING:

Note: *Appliqué and foundation blocks do not have specific cutting directions. Follow instructions on CD to prepare and sew applique and foundation blocks.*

Patchwork Blocks

Zigzag Tree

2 C squares, light blue

6 B triangles, light blue

2 D triangles, light blue

2 E squares, light blue

4 F rectangles, light blue

2 D triangles, brown

2 F rectangles, brown

12 G triangles, medium green

12 G triangles, dark green

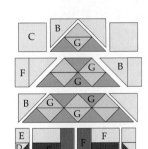

Cottage Tree

7 B triangles, medium green

1 B triangle, light green

4 B triangles, dark green

6 B triangles, light blue

4 C squares, light blue

2 F rectangles, light blue

2 F rectangles, brown

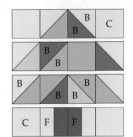

Topiary Tree

16 G triangles, medium green

14 G triangles, dark green

4 B triangles, light blue

4 C squares, light blue

4 D triangles, light blue

2 E squares, light blue

2 F rectangles, light blue

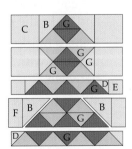

Christmas Pine Tree

5 G triangles, light green

1 G triangle, medium green

22 D triangles, light green

34 D triangles, medium green

4 B triangles, light blue

2 C squares, light blue

2 E squares, light blue

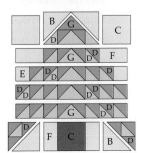

4 F rectangles, light blue

1 C square, brown

Appliqué Blocks

2 squares, 8 ½" x 8 ½", blue

Foundation-pieced Blocks

Note: *You do not have to cut exact pieces for foundation piecing.*

Finishing

6 strips, 2" x 8 ½", dark green (sashing)

4 strips, 2" x 27 ½", dark green (sashing)

2 strips, 2" x 30 ½", dark green (sashing)

2 strips, 3 ½" x 30 ½", medium green (first border - sides)

2 strips, 3 ½" x 36 ½", medium green (first border - top and bottom)

2 strips, 2" x 36 ½", dark green (second border - sides)

2 strips, 2" x 39 ½", dark green (second border - top and bottom)

4 strips, 2 ½"-wide, dark green (binding)

INSTRUCTIONS:

Patchwork Blocks

1. Referring to block diagrams 1-4, make one of each block.

2. Referring to Appliqué on the CD, make the two appliqué blocks.

4. Referring to Foundation Piecing on the CD, make the three foundation-pieced blocks

Finishing

1. Referring to photo, place blocks in three rows of three blocks.

2. Sew blocks with 2" x 8 ½" dark green sashing strips in between.

3. Sew rows together with 2" x 27 ½" dark green sashing strips in between. Sew remaing strips to sides.

4. Sew 2" x 30 ½" dark green sashing strips to top and bottom.

5. Sew first and second borders to quilt top sides first, then top and bottom.

6. Complete your quilt, referring to Finishing on the CD.

Stars and Snowflakes

Foundation Piecing and Appliqué

Approximate Size:
32 ½" x 32 ½"

Techniques:
Foundation Piecing
Appliqué

Blocks:
Six-Point Star (page 10)
Dimensional Star (page 8)
Starburst (page 22)
Star of David (page 10)
Star of Bethlehem
 (page 6)
Tumbling Snowflake
(page 15)
Snowflake (page 16)

Block Size:
8" x 8"

MATERIALS:
fat quarter each of light yellow, medium yellow, light
gold, medium gold, orange
2 yards medium blue
½ yard dark blue
1 yard backing
foundation paper
Batting1

CUTTING:
Foundation Blocks
Note: *You do not have to cut exact pieces for foundation piecing.*

Appliqué Block
1 square, 8 ½" x 8 ½", medium blue

Finishing
6 strips, 2" x 8 ½", medium blue (sashing)
4 strips, 2" x 27 ½", medium blue (sashing)
2 strips, 2" x 30 ½", medium blue (sashing)
2 strips, 2 ½" x 30 ½", dark blue (border)
2 strips, 2 ½" x 36 ½", dark blue (border)
3 strips, 2 ½"-wide, dark blue (binding)

INSTRUCTIONS:
1. Prepare Bethlehem Star pieces according to your
favorite Appliqué method on the enclosed CD and
make the appliqueé Bethlehem Star.

2. Refer to Foundation Piecing on the CD to prepare
and make the remaining foundation-pieced blocks.

3. Place blocks in 3 rows of three blocks. Sew blocks
together with 2" x 8 ½" medium blue strips in
between.

4. Sew the rows of blocks together with a 2" x
27 ½" medium blue sashing strip in between. Sew
the remaining 2" x 27 ½" red sashing strips to the side
of the quilt top.

5. Sew the 2" x 30 ½" medium blue sashing strips to
the top and bottom of the quilt.

6. Sew dark blue border to quilt top sides first, then
top and bottom.

7. Finish quilt referring to Finishing your Quilt on the
CD.

Christmas Placemats

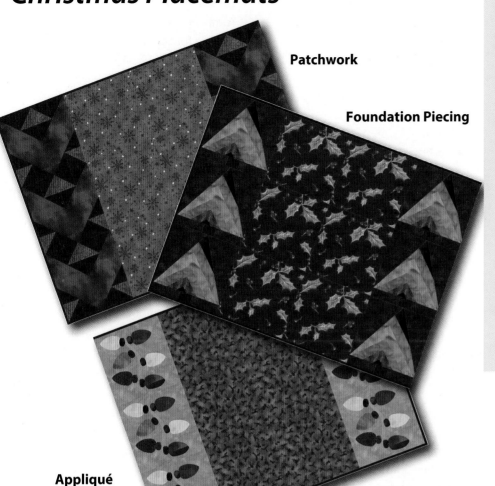

Patchwork

Foundation Piecing

Appliqué

Approximate Size:
12" x 18"

Technique:
Patchwork, Foundation Piecing, and Appliqué

Blocks:
Ribbon Border (page 50)
Log Cabin Tree (page 16)
Christmas Lights (page 19)

Block Size:
4" x 4"

MATERIALS (FOR 1 PLACEMAT)

½ yard Christmas print (center)
fat quarters of assorted Christmas fabrics
½ yard backing, binding
Batting

CUTTING (FOR 1 PLACEMAT):

one rectangle, 12 ½" x 10 ½" (center)

FINISHING

one rectangle 12 ½" x 18 ½" backing fabric
2 strips, 1 ½" x 8 ½", binding fabric

INSTRUCTIONS (FOR 1 PLACEMAT):

1. Make 6 of your favorite blocks using the 4" patterns. The blocks used in the photographed placemats are Ribbon Border, Log Cabin Tree and Christmas Lights.

2. Sew 3 blocks in a vertical strip; repeat.

3. Sew a vertical strip to sides of 12 ½" x 10 ½" rectangle.

4. Place backing wrong side up, then batting and placemat top right side up. Quilt layers together.

6. Add binding to placemat, referring to Attaching the Binding on the CD.

Index

About the CD

To run this application on Windows:

This is a self-loading CD. Simply place the CD into the CD-ROM drive. If the Auto-Run feature is not active on your system, follow these instructions to install:

• Click the Start button.

• Select Run from the menu.

• When the Run window opens, click Browse.

• Select your CD-ROM drive and then select 100 Christmas Blocks.

• Click OK and follow the onscreen instructions.

• Decide which Blocks you are making and choose the template patterns that you need to complete it; double click to open.

• If the block does not open, you may need to install Acrobat Reader. Download it easily from the internet using the website: http://www. adobe.com/products/acrobat/readstep2.html

• Print the template patterns you will need for your project.

To run this application on Mac OS 9 and OS X:

• Insert the CD into the CD-ROM drive. Double click on the *100 Christmas Blocks* icon when it appears on the desktop.

• Choose the folder name that corresponds to the section that your block is in and click to open.

• Look for the Template folder and choose the templates that you need to make your blocks.

• If the block does not open, you may need to install Acrobat Reader. Download it easily from the internet using the website: http://www. adobe.com/products/acrobat/readstep2.html

• Print the number of blocks and patterns you will need for your project.

For additional information and instructions, please read Frequently Asked Questions (FAQ.pdf) on the CD.